Happy Birthday
to Paula
April 14, 1987

With love and hugs

From Betty and Jack

WISCONSIN

WISCONSIN

Photography by
Michael Weimer

Text by
Clay Schoenfeld

SKYLINE
PRESS

Produced by Boulton Publishing Services, Inc. Toronto
Designed by Fortunato Aglialoro

©1985 Oxford University Press (Canadian Branch)
SKYLINE PRESS is a registered imprint of Oxford University Press

ISBN 0-19-540629-X
1 2 3 4 – 8 7 6 5

Printed in Hong Kong by Scanner Art Services, Inc. Toronto

INTRODUCTION

Just about everybody knows something about Wisconsin, because some Wisconsin products and people have entered the national lexicon in an indelible manner: milk, muskies, Milwaukee beer, and McCarthyism, for example; or La Follette, Lombardi, Leopold, and Laverne (and Shirley); and certainly that spritely bumper-sticker, ESCAPE TO WISCONSIN, with all the slogan conjures up in the way of susurrant wildland waters sparkling in a summer sunset.

As they sing at Wisconsin's famous fifth quarter at the end of a Badger football game in historic Camp Randall Stadium, 'When you say "Wisconsin", you've said it all!'

Perhaps more than any other state, Wisconsin is quintessentially a microcosm of America, her land and her people the epitome of forces that have shaped the country—yet with a flair for the different, too.

Wisconsin's geography is an American potpourri of ancient mountains, fruited plains, and inland oceans white with foam. Her climate promotes striking seasonal change; her flora and fauna are at once dramatic and diverse. The Wisconsin story under five flags is the American story of a kaleidoscopic tide of immigrants conquering a frontier. Her varied economic base supports a lifestyle that is both distinctive and representative. Her people have exhibited an innate independence that has made the 'Wisconsin Idea' a social statue of liberty.

To orient you to my home state, let me assume a role like that of the stage manager in *Our Town*, the well-known play and movie by Pulitzer Prizewinner Thornton Wilder (who, by the way, was born in Madison, Wisconsin).

First, then, I'd better show you how Wisconsin lies.

Wisconsin is that province north of Chicago that looks like the back of a left-hand mitten. Natural boundaries give a sense of geographic unity: to the left or west as you look at a map, the Mississippi and St Croix Rivers; to the north, Lake Superior and the Montreal and Menominee Rivers; to the right or east, Lake Michigan, with the Door County peninsula forming the thumb of the mitten. Only on the south does a man-made boundary ignore topographic features in separating Wisconsin from Illinois.

A geographer might point out that Wisconsin is located midway between the Equator and the North Pole and midway between the Prime Meridian and 180 degrees Longitude, thus placing the state in the center of the northern half of the Western Hemisphere, in the Central Standard Time Zone. As a state, Wisconsin is close to a national average in area (56 thousand square miles or 36 million acres) and in population (4.7 million).

When it comes to Wisconsin's natural history, however, 'average' is not as accurate a word as 'representative'.

Thanks to great glaciers that carved up what is now

Wisconsin in a variety of ways over eons of prehistoric time, you can find replicas of a variety of continental landscapes in modern Wisconsin. As you enter the state from the southeast, for example, you cruise through an outwash plain that looks for all the world like the flat prairies of Illinois and Iowa or the undulating grainfields of Washington's Palouse. Continuing northeast you traverse a classic terminal moraine, like that of some Mason-Dixon Line states, marked by numerous eskers, cuestas, and drumlins of glacial drift with amphitheater 'kettles' formed by the melting of huge buried ice blocks. To the east is the long, narrow Lake Michigan littoral, at its south a heavily urbanized Kenosha-Racine-Milwaukee area, contrasted sharply to the north by Maine-like Washington Island off Door County. Northwest of the Kettle Moraine is a crescent area, characterized by sharp-sided buttes and mesas standing above the almost desert-like remains of a huge glacial lake. This is ecologist Aldo Leopold's 'Sand County'. Then you break out into a high plain formed from a glacier-shorn ancient mountain range much older than the Rockies. So deep and solid is its underlying granite that the US Navy has selected it as the only site capable of bouncing an extremely low-frequency radio signal toward submarines submerged at great depths around the world. The most striking remnant of this Laurentian Range is Rib Mountain near Wausau, nearly 2,000 feet above sea level. All these highlands are a part of the true North Woods that run unbroken throughout Canada, interrupted only by the world's largest inland sea of Lake Superior, whose freight docks and Apostle Islands are indistinguishable at a casual glance from those of Puget Sound. Swinging around toward the south again, you'll come in southwestern Wisconsin to a unique geological museum, the land the ice forgot, a rugged landscape with an appearance of the Berkshires, the Catskills, or the southern Blue Ridge, known as the Driftless Area because it was untouched by the last ice age some seven-to-ten thousand

years ago, the only such non-glacial 'island' on the northern continent.

Because Wisconsin runs through 300 miles on its north-south axis, there's a good deal of variation in the weather. Along the Illinois border a summer day can be almost as hot and humid as Vicksburg, while Deer Lodge, Montana, has nothing on a winter night at Park Falls. But extremes in temperature are compensated for by stimulating seasonal régimes. Certain colors bespeak the representative diversity of Wisconsin seasons. Glistening white is the color of Wisconsin's four-to-five months of winter snow cover. It used to be that the tourist season ended on Labor Day when muskies and motel maids went into hibernation. No more. Some 200-thousand registered snowmobiles, four times that many cambered skis, and the best plowed highways in the country have now made Wisconsin a year-round resort. Spring brings the horizon-blue of wood violets, the state flower, and of 14,000 lakes heaving off their icy shackles to lie shimmering in the hesitant sunshine. There are another 2,000 trout streams, 33,000 miles of river frontage, 600 miles of Great Lakes shoreline, and two million billion gallons of ground water in four major aquifers. No wonder there are 74 different Long Lakes and 51 different Beaver Creeks in Wisconsin. Traversing the north-south axis, the Wisconsin River drains a quarter of the total area of the state. Its Indian name could have been coined by an early tourism huckster, meaning variously 'gathering of waters' or 'river of a thousand isles'. Early adventurer Pierre Radisson was to call the valley 'a laborinth of pleasure'. In summer, green grows the alfalfa, clover, and corn in the valleys of America's Dairyland, and in the uplands the pine, fir, spruce, hemlock, birch, and 'popple' on two and one-half million acres of state and county forests. Autumn brings the yellow, amber, and scarlet of aspen, oak, hickory, and maple; the red lanterns and smoky gold of Leopold's blackberry bushes and tamarack; the cardinal of 75-thousand Badger football fans 'getting the red out' on a fall weekend; and the blaze orange of nearly ten times that many hunters in pursuit of a million whitetail deer in unnumbered Wisconsin swamps at dawn the third Saturday in November.

As you might surmise, Wisconsin's geography and climate have conspired to provide a haven for a scintillating range of native vegetation and wildlife. Three are particularly noteworthy tributes to a fortunate strain of conservation in Wisconsin hearts.

First, the remnant 1,200 acres of native prairie preserved (as by a miracle and by periodic controlled burning) in the University of Wisconsin Arboretum at Madison: a tiny sea of the yellow puccoon, adropogen, compass plant, pasque flower, silky aster, grama grass, bluestem, wild indigo, rattlesnake master, and panic grass that once tickled the bellies of buffalo or hid beyond sight the yearling oxen of pioneers. Second, the Dodge-County-wide expanse of Horicon Marsh, preserved by the tax dollars of countless duck hunters, and now harboring the sensational sight of a quarter-million Canada geese on their semi-annual skyborn journey, their haunting cry coming down from twilight heights to stir the human breast as does no other outdoor sound. Third, America's largest and fiercest fresh-water game fish, the huge (up to 60 pounds), voracious muskellunge, or musky, at home in northern Wisconsin waters as nowhere else, to the tune of some 70,000 taken annually—in part, perhaps because the Wisconsin Department of Natural Resources rears and stocks many times that number each year, and because if a musky isn't almost a yard long it isn't a 'keeper'.

Now, says our *Stage Manager*, about the human history of Wisconsin.

The story of Wisconsin is in a way the story of America in miniature, as historian H. Russel Austin has observed.

Native Americans came here first across a land bridge from Asia to do battle with mastodons and mammoths in the era of the last glaciers. By the time of the white man's coming, what is now Wisconsin was the home of Chippewa, Dakota, Fox, Huron, Illinois, Massacouten, Menominee, Miami, Oneida, Ottowa, Potawatomi, Sauk, and Winnebago.

Wisconsin white man's history, like America's, reflects the European powers' struggle for colonial territory, and the region that is now the state was ruled successively by three countries: Spain, France, and Great Britain—until the 'Stars and Stripes' was run up in 1783.

Although the Pope had technically given Spain dominion over what is now Wisconsin in the 16th century, Jean Nicolet of France was the first Caucasian actually to set foot in the state—in 1634. As Christopher Columbus of Genoa had sailed the Atlantic to the new world, Nicolet sailed across Lake Michigan and stepped ashore on Green Bay. We are told that both Columbus and Nicolet made their voyages under the same delusion—just beyond the water barrier they had crossed lay the Orient. Hence the elaborate silk robes Nicolet wore as he disembarked from his birchbark canoe—to be greeted by startled Winnebagoes.

Making a much less dramatic entrance to Green Bay in 1959 was an Italian explorer who was to discover how to take a foundering, publicly-owned pro-football team to the pinnacle of Super Bowl success in the 1960s. Vince Lombardi may never actually have said that 'winning isn't everything, it's the only thing,' but his spirit and that of his legendary Green Bay Packers live on in 'Titletown, USA.'

The eastern lakeshore of Wisconsin, like the eastern seaboard of the United States, was the first to be explored and mapped, and was the site of the earliest white settlements, but the restless tides of migration soon led to the charting and settlement of western lands, as they did through America as a whole. Joliet and Marquette pushed on to identify Wisconsin's western bordering waterway, the upper Mississippi, in 1673, in a parallel to Lewis and Clark's later expedition to the Pacific

Coast of the United States.

As the eastern seaboard of the United States early became an important commercial and industrial area, so on Wisconsin's eastern lakeshore a similar development occurred, notably at Milwaukee, originally a fur-trading station. In mining, however, the lead region of southwest Wisconsin drew settlers as early as the 1820s, in a parallel to the Gold Rush to the West two decades later. Pioneer Cornish miners wintered in shallow shafts like so many badgers, from which comes Wisconsin's nickname.

The first permanent settlers and community builders in New England were predominantly of Anglo-Saxon stock. Similarly, descendants of those Yankees played a leading role in the early settlement and development of Wisconsin. Later came waves of immigrants, past Ellis Island and on to Wisconsin—Germans, Swiss, Irish, and Norwegians, Poles, Swedes, and Italians, Danes, Dutch, and Finns, and dozens of other nationalities, and so on to the recent 'boat people'. Today Wisconsin, like America, is a hybrid culture, richer and more vigorous than any single strain. Yet Wisconsin continues to revel annually in such rich ethnic heritage celebrations as Stoughton's Syttendai Mai, New Glarus' Wilhelm Tell Festival, Cedar Grove's Holland Days, Cable's Birkebeiner, Milwaukee's Holiday Folk Fair, and Black River Falls' Indian Pow Wow. The whole polyglot panorama is preserved at Old World Wisconsin near Eagle, a 600-acre outdoor museum of 19th century Wisconsin.

Originally a part of the Old Northwest Territory and later a part of the Territories of Indiana, Illinois, and Michigan, Wisconsin gained Territorial status in its own right in 1836 and statehood in 1848.

For important political and educational experiments, Wisconsin has been the laboratory of America. The Republican party, through which the abolitionist movement won its victory nationally, was founded at Ripon, Wisconsin, early in 1854. Progressivism, a national political movement largely conceived and led by the elder Robert M. La Follette, had its roots in Wisconsin. During the first 40 years of this century, no state in the Union has pioneered more innovative, enduring legislation and public service practices than has Wisconsin: direct primary elections, non-partisan municipal elections, a civil service system, workers' and unemployment compensation; public regulation of banks, utilities, and railroads; factory safety legislation, limited working hours for women and children, a state income tax, forest reserve acts, laws fostering farm cooperatives, a league of women voters, a kindergarten program, a vocational-school system, university extension agents, university faculty members as government advisors, a ringing statement of academic freedom—all this is the 'Wisconsin Idea'. So Wisconsin state government today, in the words of Professor Robert C. Nesbit, is 'the inheritor of a proud tradition; it defines a level of expectation in terms of honesty, competence, human motivation, and service' that sets a national standard of excellence, perhaps best signified by the magic mile of State Street in Madison that links a proud State Capitol and her 'Miss Forward' statue with a world-class University whose campus boundaries are those of the state itself—and beyond.

The nation's wars also have linked Wisconsin to the rest of America. Charles de Langlade and his Wisconsin Indians sacking General Braddock (and his aide George Washington) along the Monongahela in 1755. The Iron Brigade at Antietam and Gettysburg. Cordelia Harvey, 'Wisconsin angel of the battlefield', in what was to become the American Red Cross. The Red Arrow Division in the Meuse-Argonne. General Billy Mitchell warning in 1935 of a surprise attack on Pearl Harbor. Over 330,000 Badgers serving in uniform around the globe in WW II. The first General MacArthur making history at Missionary Ridge in 1863, his son at Inchon in 1950. The bombing of a UW campus building in 1970 dramatizing

American anti-Vietnam fervor.

Our 'Stage Manager' reminds us that Wisconsin's current lifestyle rests securely on four diverse economic bases—manufacturing, tourism, agriculture, and the service sector.

For a state exhibiting such bucolic charm, it may be surprising that Wisconsin ranks around 10th or 12th among the States in the value of goods her factories turn out annually, and her products themselves are surprisingly diverse. You're familiar with many of the range of trade names: heavy machinery like giant turbines and nuclear reactors from Allis-Chalmers, Bucyrus-Erie land machines, Nordberg diesels, Giddings and Lewis machine tools, and Heil vans; processed foods like Oscar Meyer wieners, Jones sausages, Green Giant peas, and Frito snacks; paper products like Kleenex and Charmin (if all the pulpwood used in a year by the state's mills were loaded on railroad cars, it would take a fast freight train a month to pass a given point); transportation equipment like Chevrolets, Alliances, FWD trucks, J.I. Case tractors, John Deere snowmobiles, Mercury outboard motors, Johnson and Thompson boats, and Harley Davidson motorcycles; electrical and electronic equipment like Trane air-conditioners, Johnson temperature controls, Speed Queen and Hotpoint washers, and A.O. Smith water heaters; printing and publishing like books and games from Western; lumber from Goodman, Connor, and Weyerhaeuser; exotic chemicals from Ansul; aluminumware like Mirro; plumbing fixtures from Kohler; Briggs and Stratton small engines, AC sparkplugs, Flambeau plastics, Johnson wax, Parker pens, Jacobsen lawnmowers, Ray-o-Vac batteries, Freeman shoes, Oshkosh B' Gosh overalls—indeed an industrial pattern of striking complexity; and, of course, the beers that make Milwaukee famous (not to mention La Crosse, Monroe, Stevens Point, Eau Claire, and Chippewa Falls; collectively Wisconsin's breweries bottle, can, or barrel enough beer a year to float a battleship, or at least to make it stagger). Lead and zinc mining is no more in southwestern Wisconsin, but very valuable are the massive sand and gravel deposits found throughout the state in glacial outwash formations. Recently discovered zinc and copper deposits in northern Wisconsin may prove extractable if Exxon can pass a rigid environmental-impact test. Shipbuilding and commercial fishing on the Great Lakes add to Wisconsin's diverse industrial base. On the horizon are high-tech industries fostered by University of Wisconsin research, for example in the field of genetic engineering.

Nurtured by those multi-million acres of lakes, the hospitality, travel, and recreation business is second in economic rank in Wisconsin. About 13 per cent of the state's work force is employed playing host. Tourism statistics are mind-boggling. For example, Wisconsin's 55 state parks draw 10 million visitors a year and her 9 state forests another 4.5 million. Two million people buy fishing licenses to catch 68 million fish a year; another million buy hunting licenses to bag 5 million game birds and animals. More than a half-million boats ply Wisconsin waters. To help maintain her natural amenities, Wisconsin has added over 400 thousand public acres since 1969 and spent some 250 million dollars on water pollution abatement under her unique Outdoor Recreation Act Program alone. Even the State Supreme Court has backstopped tourism. In a landmark 1952 decision the Court decreed: 'The right of citizens to enjoy our navigable waters for recreational purposes, including the enjoyment of scenic beauty, is a legal right that is entitled to all the protection which is given financial rights.' And many resort owners have cooperated by voluntarily limiting advertising signs to the very discreet black-and-white arrows that mark crossroads all around the Rhinelander region.

It is no idle boast that Wisconsin's auto license plates read, 'America's Dairyland'. Wisconsin is No. 1 in the country in the production of milk, butter, cheese, buttermilk, condensed milk, and milk cows. Fluid milk production alone is 23,800,000,000 pounds a year. Packaged in one-quart cartons and stacked side by side, that milk would form 28 rows from New York to San Francisco. (By the way, if you look at one of those cartons, it may say 'whole homogenized'. How do you know it's whole? Because a University of Wisconsin chemist perfected a simple test for measuring the butterfat content of milk. That carton probably also says something like 'fortified with vitamin D' because another U W chemist discovered a way to impart to milk that otherwise rare bone-building vitamin.)

But Wisconsin agriculture is more than dairy cows. The state is No. 1 or No. 2 in the production of carrots, snap beans, hay, peas, sweet corn, ginseng, and cranberries. Wisconsin also produces its share of beef cattle, hogs, chickens, ducks, turkeys, honey, maple syrup, lima beans, cucumbers for pickles, beets for canning, cabbage for kraut, potatoes, and tobacco, on the 88-thousand-some farms that punctuate the landscape. If a smoke-stack is synonymous with Pittsburgh, a silo is certainly a symbol of Wisconsin.

Wisconsin's service industry sector is dominated by big insurance companies. You've undoubtedly heard of some of them: Northwestern Mutual (the quiet company), Employers' Mutual (of Wausau, spelled W-A-U-S-A-U), Sentry, and Cuna (Credit Union National Association) Mutual. Because of its historic educational, economic, and social roles, state government is also big business in Wisconsin. But Wisconsin is traditionally a pay-as-you-go state, with a lower debt ratio than others. It scores high in terms of labor skills and an assurance that the tax dollar is honestly spent. For example, Wisconsin is among the lowest in the ratio of state employees per 1,000 citizens. Half of Wisconsin's people have prudently invested in 104 state and federal savings and loan associations with current assets of $15 billion.

Someone in the audience just asked the *Our Town* stage manager, 'How about culture and love of beauty?'

Out of the bustle of Wisconsin's diverse culture has risen a respectable number of artists of high national reputation—humanists, writers, designers, creators of paintings and sculpture, music and drama, many of them influenced by the state's distinctive landscape, and many in turn the recipients of University of Wisconsin honors: historians like Frederick Jackson Turner, Frederic L. Paxton, Louise P. Kellogg, Merle Curti, Marshall Clagett; poet Ella Wheeler Wilcox; authors like Hamlin Garland, Zona Gale, Edna Ferber, Glenway Wescott, August Derleth, Mark Schorer, Emily Hahn, Eudora Welty, Margery Kinnan Rawlings, Edward Harris Heth, Herbert O. Kubly, Sterling North, Helen C. White; exponent of organic architecture Frank Lloyd Wright; artists Richard Lorenz, John Steuart Curry, Aaron Bohrod, Georgia O'Keefe, James Watrous, John Wilde; playwrights Nat Hiken, Howard Teichman, Lorraine Hansberry, Jerry McNeely; photographer Edward Steichen; dancer Margaret H. Doubler; sculptors Vinnie Ream, Helen Farsworth Mears; music makers Carrie Jacobs Bond, Liberace, Hildegarde, Les Paul and Mary Ford, Gunnar Johanssen; show biz figures like Alfred Lunt and Lynn Fontanne, Alan Schneider, Fredric March, Don Ameche, Spencer Tracy, Tom Ewell, Gilda Gray, Pat O'Brien, Fred MacMurray, Gale Sondergaard, Colleen Dewhurst, Orson Welles, Uta Hagen, Gena Rowlands, Tom Hulce, Daniel J. Travanti, Carl Laemmle, Gene Wilder, Dennis Morgan, Harrison Ford, Allan Mandel, Jane Kazmarek, Lisabeth Bartlett, Rusty Lemorande; conservation penmen John Muir, Aldo Leopold, Sigurd Olson, and Dion Henderson; the circus magnate Ringling Brothers; media persons like top-drawer journalists Louis P. Lochner, Marquis Childs, Hans V. Kaltenborn, Leonard Silk, Edwin Newman; syndicated columnists Ann Landers and Bill Stokes; TV personalities Gary Bender and Mack Anderson; Professors Earl Terry and Edward Bennett who launched the oldest radio station in the nation (WHA);

public broadcasting's William G. Harley; *Look*'s Dan Mich; crusading editor William T. Evjue of the (Madison) *Capital Times*; and the staffers of the employee-owned *Milwaukee Journal*, traditionally a district attorney for the people of the state.

Other stage managers could list other names.

Can Wisconsin maintain its intriguing blend of business and the bucolic? That's a good question. The four P's of a domestic Apocalypse threaten Wisconsin as they do the rest of the country—population pressures, toxic piles, pollution, and the proclivities of some people toward irrational consumption.

Wisconsin has a couple of features going for it, however. First, two-thirds of the state's population is concentrated in the lower eastern third of the state, as if a recent glacier had deposited a human moraine, leaving the upper two-thirds of the state comparatively underdeveloped, a northern highland with more starlit nights and remote campsites than neon and parking meters. Second, the name Wisconsin has become practically synonymous over the years with resource development linked to environmental husbandry, or *vice versa*. As her conservation poet laureate suggested:

'We shall hardly relinquish the steam shovel, which after all has many good points; what we seek are gentler and more objective criteria for its successful use.'

Aldo Leopold called that philosophy an 'ecological conscience'. If such a *modus operandi* is alive and well anywhere, it is to be found in Wisconsin. To be successful today no Wisconsin politician can run on anything but a platform pledged to the preservation of the 'integrity, stability, and beauty' of the Wisconsin community, and that community 'includes the soil, water, fauna, and flora—as well as people.'

Maybe this is the right moment to conclude with a paraphrase from *Our Town*:

As you can see, we've got a lot of pleasures of a particular kind in Wisconsin. We like the sun coming up over a lake in the morning, and we all notice a good deal about birds. We pay a lot of attention to them. In the silence of a smog-free night, we watch the stars doing their old crisscross journeys in the sky. And we enjoy the change of seasons; yes, everybody knows about them...in Wisconsin.

CLAY SCHOENFELD

1 For the multitudes of people who come to Wisconsin every year from the direction of Chicagoland, it is a Walworth County scene like this that greets them first. The southeastern corner of the state is a part of the nation's lush cornbelt. The lone open-grown oak here is a vestige of what Wisconsin-born naturalist John Muir called the 'sunny oak openings' that the first pioneers of the region found in the 1830s.

2 What more fitting portrait with which to introduce a book about Wisconsin! Meet the real 'Miss Wisconsin', a handsome heifer dairy cow (in this case a Jersey). Wisconsin is hands-down America's Dairyland, No. 1 among the states in the production of milk, butter, cheese, buttermilk, condensed milk, and milk cows.

3 *(right)* Another Walworth County farm just north of the Illinois border. There is a special spirit in the outdoor air of early August in Wisconsin. Nature pauses. August dawns are moist, and fog fingers hover over prairie pastures, spangled with cobwebs. By noon an occasional vagrant wind will wave the woods and sweep with shadowy gust a field of corn.

4 *(left)* The green, green farm-fields of Green County. Farms cover more than half of Wisconsin's total land area, and more than a third of the labor force produces or markets farm products.

5 When you think of Wisconsin, you probably think of cheese. This is the 'Wheel of Swiss Chateau' cheese shop in Monroe, the cheese capital of Wisconsin.

6 As at Walworth County's fair at Elkhorn, harness-racing is a popular summer pastime in Wisconsin. But there's no pari-mutual betting!

7 *(right)* More than most states, Wisconsin was a great melting pot of immigrants from many lands, and their modern-day descendants like to keep alive their varied ethnic heritages. Here the Stoughton High School Norwegian Dancers perform at an annual Syttende Mai Festival in Dane County in May.

8 *Viola*, violet, the Wisconsin state flower, seen here in Lafayette County. There are actually 21 species of the genus to be found in Wisconsin. The most common is *V. papilionacea*, found everywhere—in borders of woods, meadows, roadsides, and near dwellings. It is often planted on city lots. Many color variations appear, from the classic violet to white with blue veins or blue speckles.

9 *(right)* Situated on a peninsula between two lakes, Wisconsin's capital city of Madison presents a striking skyline approached from any direction. As Longfellow once wrote in tribute: 'All like a floating landscape seems, in cloudland or a land of dreams.'

10 Wisconsin has sent more than her share of citizens to the nation's wars. Some Wisconsin regiments in the Civil War were made up of nationality groups. The 15th Infantry was largely Norwegian, under young Colonel Hans Christian Heg, former state prison commissioner, the first Norwegian to hold a state office in the United States. The 15th fought in 26 battles. Colonel Heg was mortally wounded at Chickamauga. His statue stands in the State Capitol Square at Madison.

11 (right) What has been called 'a masterpiece of ceiling decoration' adorns the dome some 250 feet above the rotunda of the Wisconsin State Capitol Building in Madison. Called by artist Edwin Howland Blashfield 'The Resources of Wisconsin', a 13-foot-high central figure symbolizes Wisconsin enthroned upon clouds and wrapped in the folds of the American flag, holding a scepter of wheat. Around and below her are female figures bearing up specimens of such Wisconsin products as lead, copper, tobacco, fruit, freshwater pearl. The building was completed in 1917. There are daily guided tours.

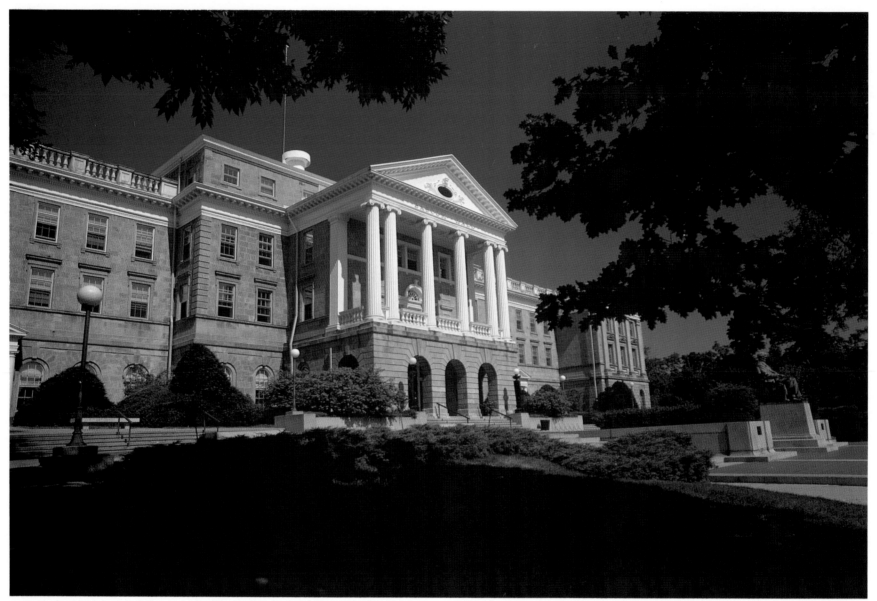

12 Lincoln Terrace and Bascom Hall atop Bascom Hill in Madison, the heart of the University of Wisconsin System, one of the ten largest and most distinguished in the country, serving over 160,000 students on 26 campuses throughout the state. Bolted to the Hall is a plaque bearing a famous 1894 Board of Regents pledge to 'ever encourage that continual and fearless sifting and winnowing by which alone the truth can be found.'

13 *(right)* The special home of the Badgerland spirit may well be Camp Randall Stadium at Madison, especially in that spent and sacred moment between the halves of a University of Wisconsin-Madison football game, when the partisan crowd rises to sing that mighty hymn, 'Varsity'.

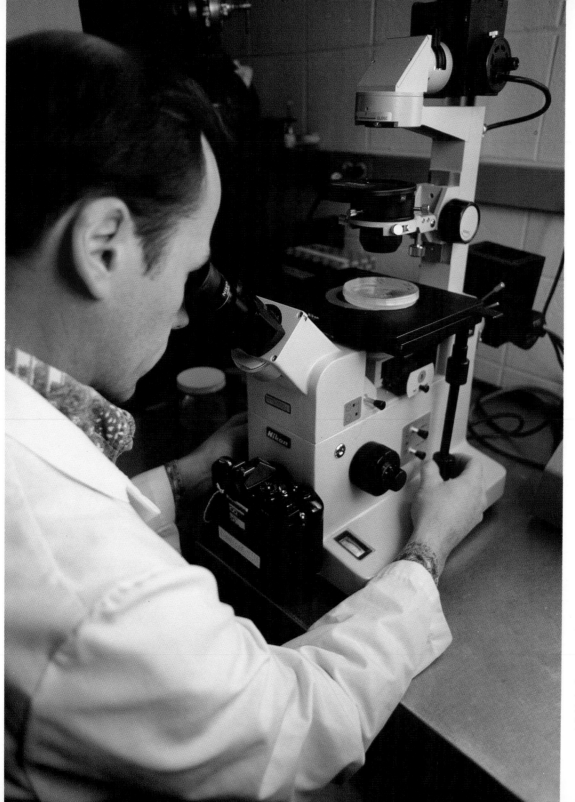

14 In a University of Wisconsin-Madison horticulture laboratory, Professor Brent McCown experiments with micropropagation — clonal propagation of plants from tissue cultured in a sterile test-tube environment — to cut down the time and the uncertainty in tree improvement programs. In both the size of its multi-million dollar annual research budget and the number of its discoveries that have improved the human condition, UW-Madison is a world leader among research universities.

15 No, this is not a scene on the Riviera or even at Newport Beach, even though it may look like a resort. It is actually the Lake Mendota shore of the campus of the University of Wisconsin-Madison, a haven for students escaping from classes in one of the 10 largest summer sessions in the country. As you might imagine, Mendota in turn is one of the most studied lakes in the world, a cradle of the science of limnology.

16 On 576 rolling acres of wooded farmland near Eagle in southeastern Wisconsin, the lives and buildings of Wisconsin's ethnic pioneers have been painstakingly re-created and brought vividly to life. At Old World Wisconsin you can really go back into time, as here inside a 19th-century schoolhouse. Wisconsin was the home of the first kindergarten in the country and one of the first free public schools outside of New England.

17 In 1850 Americans were on their way west. They traveled by canal boat and lake steamer, by horse, oxcart, on foot, and by train. After arriving from Pennsylvania, Sylvanus Wade and his family walked down an Indian trail until they found their place in Wisconsin history. They helped build the plank road between Fond du Lac and Sheboygan, and mid-way at Greenbush they erected a large inn to serve passers-by. Today at restored Wade House you can step back into time and refresh yourself as travelers have been doing for over 130 years.

18 *(left)* The entrance to the picturesque Wollersheim Winery at Prairie du Sac. Count Agoston Harazsthy first harvested grapes here in the 1840 s, and then moved west to found the California wine industry.

19 Not a castle on the Rhine but Holy Hill Monastery atop a moraine in Washington County. There's a little bit of all the world in Wisconsin.

20 The lovely pasque flower (*Anemone patens*) is of the very spirit of spring in Wisconsin, appearing as early as late March, as here in the Southern Kettle Moraine State Forest in Waukesha County. Though they seem too delicate to survive a June breeze, the lovely purplish or blue-to-white petals bloom all through the winds of April.

21 *(right)* One of the great outdoor experiences in the country is to be had at the Horicon Marsh National and State Wildlife Refuges in central Wisconsin, where each spring and fall upwards of a quarter-million Canada geese (*Branta canadensis interior*) stop over on their semi-annual migration. Fifty years ago Horicon was a bone-dry monument to misguided agriculture. Then came conservation-minded sportsmen. Armed with a Supreme Court decision, they plugged drainage ditches, built dams, and planted food patches. Today in the environs of Horicon you can see as many geese in a day as your forefathers saw in a year.

22 The marina at Lakeside Park on Lake Winnebago at Fond du Lac. The French traders who first came to the region from the north referred to it as the *fond*, or farther end, of the lake; hence the name Fond du Lac.

23 *(right)* Another marina, this one at High Cliff State Park, with Lake Winnebago in the background. Winnebago is Wisconsin's largest interior lake. Legendary lumberjack Paul Bunyan is said to have scooped it out as a watering trough for Babe, his big blue ox. Today more than half-a-million boats of all shapes and sizes ply Wisconsin's extensive waterways.

24 *(left)* A winter landscape near Ironton in Sauk County. As Wisconsin ecologist Aldo Leopold once wrote: 'There is much confusion between land and country. Land is the place where corn, gullies, and mortgages grow. Country is the personality of the land, the collective harmony of its soil, life, and weather. . . . Poor land may be rich country. . . . Only economists mistake physical opulence for riches.'

25 A newspaper correspondent stood on the Milwaukee docks in 1843 and wrote: 'The torrent of immigration swells very strongly . . . The refugees arrive daily in their national dresses. . . . Here, on the pier, I see disembarking the Germans, the Norwegians, the Swedes, the Swiss, the Irish.' Today the evidence of that great migration is everywhere throughout Wisconsin. This is the interior of the Moravian Church at Heritage Hill State Park near Green Bay.

26 The Wisconsin River valley as seen from Gibraltar Rock near Lodi in Dane County. The Wisconsin is the state's principal interior river, draining a quarter of the state. To the state it bequeathed its Indian name, translated as 'gathering of waters' or 'river of a thousand isles.'

27 *(right)* A slalom skier rockets down Cascade Mountain near Portage in Columbia County. More than 50 ski areas in Wisconsin offer complete facilities for a ski vacation; many others provide just a slope and the snow. Cross-country skiing has swept the state, both as a participatory and a spectator sport. Ice fishing, ice boating, and snowmobiling are other popular winter pastimes.

28 The Vince Lombardi Gallery in the Green Bay Packer Hall of Fame at Green Bay. It's possible more people identify Wisconsin with the football Packers than with any other Wisconsin product. Green Bay is the smallest city in the country to hold a professional sport franchise. The Packers are publicly owned and patriotically supported. If you want to buy a season ticket to home games, they'll add you to a 20,000-name waiting list.

29 In the summer of 1883 five Baraboo, Wisconsin, brothers put on their first professional circus performances. They made $300, bought a wagon, a trained horse, and a dancing bear and went on the road. In 1906 Charles, Albert, Alfred, Otto, and John Ringling bought out the Barnum & Bailey circus to become 'the greatest show on earth'. No other 'live' theatrical production has ever been witnessed by so many people. Today the Circus World Museum at Baraboo preserves the memories of the Ringlings and of the dozen other circuses spawned in Wisconsin—with spectacular big-top performances, wild animals, parades, colorful circus wagons, rousing calliope music, clowns, and cotton candy.

30 (left) At Devil's Lake State Park in Sauk County, fishermen are dwarfed by the remains of a natural cataclysm of eons ago. Beginning in the 1890s Wisconsin citizens believed they should have scenic areas 'for the use and inspiration of the people'. Today Wisconsin's 55 state parks draw 10 million visitors a year. To camp at Devil's Lake on a popular weekend, better make reservations months ahead of time.

31 Devil's Doorway, one of the many striking rock formations at Devil's Lake State Park. Dramatic glacial action in the ancient Baraboo Mountain Range ripped away huge blocks of quartzite rock, deposited moraines, and formed cliffbound Devil's Lake.

32 *(left)* Aptly named Mirror Lake in Mirror Lake State Park near Lake Delton in Sauk County. Nearby is famous Wisconsin Dells, a beautifully carved gorge of the Wisconsin River, produced when the last glacier changed the course of the river, and in melting poured into it great volumes of rapidly moving water, which cut a deep channel in the sedimentary rock. Throngs come each summer night to see the ceremonial performed in a natural amphitheater by Native Americans high above the river they named.

33 Fruit-growing is a surprising aspect of Wisconsin agriculture. The Wollersheim Winery at Prairie du Sac in Sauk County is the only winery in the state that grows its own grapes, carrying on a great German tradition.

34 Consolidated Papers Inc., at Wisconsin Rapids, manufactures coated paper for nine out of the ten top national magazines as well as some of the finest commercial printing papers in use today. The wood-products industry is Wisconsin's second-largest employer, next only to metal-working.

35 The soils of the old Glacial Lake Wisconsin in the middle of the state used to be too thin to support farming until University agricultural scientists learned how to irrigate and fertilize. Now the 'golden sands' of Marathon and adjoining counties are the heart of a significant potato-growing and potato-chip-making empire.

36 The valley of the Wisconsin River seen from a bluff across from Prairie du Sac in Sauk County. This was the setting for the novels of Wisconsin's most prolific writer, August Derleth, in his marathon Sac Prairie Saga. Derleth also wrote the definitive book on the Wisconsin River.

37 *(right)* Looking northward from Mill Bluff in Mill Bluff State Park near Fort McCoy in Monroe County. This is the 'coulee country' made famous by turn-of-the-century author Hamlin Garland, where steep-sided hills and hidden valleys alternate with swamplands. McCoy is the summer home of Wisconsin's 32nd National Guard Brigade, the 'Red Arrow' outfit of Argonne and Buna fame.

38 *(left)* Hope springs eternal for these pier fishermen at dusk in Ephraim harbor, Door County. Founded in 1853 by Moravians from Norway, Ephraim is a resort village well known for its Scandinavian Fyr-Bal Fest and Regatta. A monument to the Moravian founders overlooks the harbor.

39 The inner workings of the Pabst Brewery in Milwaukee, the beer capital of the world. Surprisingly enough, it was three Welshmen who built Wisconsin's first brewery—in Milwaukee naturally—in 1840. They were rapidly overtaken by a quartet of German brewers—Pabst, Blatz, Miller, and Schlitz. Today the G. Heileman Brewing Company of La Crosse, Wisconsin, is on an equal par, thanks to the groundwater of surpassing quality and quantity that news-media advertising tells us all about. The baseball Brewers may be better known country-wide now than any other Milwaukee product.

40 Hay bales dot farm fields in Shawano County. Wisconsin leads the country in the production of hay, a necessary winter forage for dairy cows. Alfalfa, clover, and timothy are the most common components.

41 *(right)* Hikers wander a state-supervised trail in Door County's Peninsula State Park. 'This thing called "nature study"', wrote Aldo Leopold, 'despite the shivers it brings to the spines of the elect, constitutes the first embryonic groping of the mass mind toward perception. The outstanding characteristic of perception is that it entails no consumption and no dilution of the resources.'

42 *(left)* Maritime graffiti on the Anderson Dock building in Ephraim on the Door County peninsula that separates Green Bay from Lake Michigan—a suggestion of the New England shore.

43 Indian Summer, Door County. It is hard to imagine what Wisconsin would be like without autumn. Other climes may see summer slip into winter with only a whimpering rain to mark the passage. But in Wisconsin summer dies with a flourish. From hills aflame with the scarlet and saffron of sumac and maple, from marshes glowing with the frosty purple of asters and gentian, October calls with insistent voice.

44 *(left)* Pleasure boats docked at Door County's Fish Creek on Green Bay. Sheltered coves provide fine natural harbors on the western side of the peninsula, augmented by the town's marina. The Peninsula Players, designated the oldest resident summer stock company in the county by the Actors Equity Association, perform nightly in season.

45 The Coast Guard station at the end of the breakwater at Milwaukee harbor on Lake Michigan. The deep-draft St Lawrence Seaway, opened in mid-1959, made the Great Lakes in effect the fourth seacoast of the United States. Milwaukee has an international reputation as the best-equipped heavy-lift port on the Great Lakes and the Seaway. Milwaukee's diversified factories consume more steel than those of any other city in the United States.

46 A City Hall clock tower dominates downtown Milwaukee, Wisconsin's metropolis. The scene is abundantly familiar to viewers of those popular TV situation comedies, *Laverne and Shirley* and *Happy Days*, now enjoying extended reruns. Native-born stars of another era, Jack Carson and Dennis Morgan, made the movie 'Two Guys from Milwaukee.'

47 Milwaukee's eclectic blend of varied architecture and recreational parks is evident in this view of the northeast portion of the city. Someday somebody ought to write a big-time song about Milwaukee.

48 A Milwaukee Mitchell Park pond picks up the reflection of a horticultural dome of the Mitchell Park Conservatory. Three glass domes, each seven stories high, house a tropical exhibit, a desert exhibit, and special themed floral displays, particularly spectacular at Easter and Christmas.

49 Boats docked at Door County's Fish Creek. The Peninsula Music Festival, Wisconsin's premier classical music event, is held in Fish Creek every August.

50 If there's another home of the Badgerland spirit, it's at the Wisconsin State Fair, held each August in West Allis, a western suburb of Milwaukee, where Wisconsin kids of all ages from seven to seventy revel in carnival rides and prize cows.

51 (right) The Milwaukee County Zoo has one of the country's largest and most comprehensive collections. Animals are displayed in five continental groupings and in natural habitat settings which give the illusion that predator and prey are together. This, of course, is a polar bear.

52 Cherries for baking, picked by hand in one of Door County's fabulous orchards.

53 *(right)* Mint-fresh Alliance automobiles awaiting shipment to dealerships from the American Motors assembly plant at Kenosha. From hand-held snowblowers to huge earthmovers, Wisconsin produces more internal combustion engines than any state in the country—in striking contrast to her reputation as only an agricultural area.

54 *(left)* A dramatic sunrise over Cana Island, off a point of land near Bailey's Harbor, the oldest village in Door County, founded by fishermen in 1851. The Island Lighthouse, built that year, is still in service.

55 Anglers begin their day on one of the manifold lakes in the Nicolet National Forest of northern Wisconsin. The region is particularly famous as the watery retreat of the state fish *Esox masquinongy*, the muskellunge or musky, a large American pike much sought-after by fishers because it can reach a weight of some 60 pounds.

56 Rich fall foliage as seen from the lookout tower atop Rib Mountain near Wausau, at nearly 2,000 feet above sea level one of the highest remnants of the ancient Laurentian Shield, much older than the Rockies.

57 A Rusk County dairy herd. Add 300 billion tons of rich soil to a moderately flat landscape and a moderate climate with plenty of water, and you get ideal conditions for dairy and vegetable farming.

58 *(left)* An almost-unbelievable two million people buy fishing licenses to catch 68 million fish a year in Wisconsin, as here at the Lac Vieux Desert spillway north of Phelps in storied Vilas County.

59 A snow-covered hiking trail on Rib Mountain in Marathon County. In Wisconsin a winter walk has an appeal all its own—bright berries against soft evergreens, hardy winter birds, animal tracks, the squeak of L.L. Bean pacs on complaining snow. A January trudge can clear cluttered minds and present a clean, white page on which to draft the story of another year.

60 Lac Vieux Desert, straddling the Wisconsin-Michigan border, is the modest source of the mighty Wisconsin River, with its power dams, factories, and stretches of turbulent canoe water sometimes called 'the hardest working river in the world'.

61 *(right)* Moonrise over Little John Junior Lake at dusk in the Northern Highlands State Forest west of Sayner. How did Wisconsin wind up with 15,000-some lakes? That's easy. They are nothing more nor less than the footprints of giant lumberjack Paul Bunyan, left in the spring of the year when the ground was soft. (And if you believe that, you're a candidate for membership in the famous Burlington, Wisconsin, Liars' Club!)

62 *(left)* Autumn colors and a rowboat reflected in a still Tomahawk River near the city of Tomahawk in Lincoln County. The nomenclature of Native Americans and of our first martyred President are intermingled in Wisconsin history.

63 One of Wisconsin's many Bass Lakes, and Timm's Hill, the true highest point in the state, near Ogema, in Price County.

64 Flourishing birch trees reach for the sky in the Chequamegon National Forest in Washburn County. This was once the 'cutover', so savaged by lumbering and forest fires as to resemble a moonscape. Today Wisconsin is green again, thanks to far-sighted reforestation taxes and laws, and to a new breed of lumberman, the professional forester. Each year three state tree-nurseries produce over 18 million seedlings, and commercial foresters practice sustained-yield cutting.

65 (right) The start of the American Birkebeiner XII cross-country ski race near Cable and Hayward in northwestern Wisconsin. The 'Birkie' is North America's largest cross-country event, drawing thousands of participants annually from all over the world.

66 A secluded lake along Pallette Lake Trail in the Northern Highland State Forest. Wisconsin's nine state forests attract 4.5 million visitors a year to their matchless array of hunting, fishing, camping, hiking, swimming, and birdwatching opportunities. It's estimated that three-fourths of Wisconsin's population pursues Wisconsin's wildlife with cameras, binoculars, birdfood, or guns.

67 Along Highway 131 in Vernon County, a region that could have been
the setting for 'Germelshausen' or 'Brigadoon', the mythical Old World
countrysides that came alive only once in a hundred years to succor star-
crossed lovers.

68 *(left)* As Aldo Leopold observed: 'In a country, as in people, a plain exterior often conceals hidden riches, to perceive which requires much living in and with.' This is autumn in southern Wisconsin's rural Iowa County, the author's home stomping-ground.

69 Colorful, controversial, unpredictable, and flamboyant, Wisconsin's great native-born architect, Frank Lloyd Wright, was a titan in his time—the high priest of functionalism in building design. 'A house,' he said, 'should be a circumstance in Nature, like a rock or tree.' A shining example is his own home, Taliesin, folded into the southern Wisconsin hills near Spring Green.

70 Pendarvis, a group of restored Cornish miners' homes built nearly 150 years ago, recalls the days when Mineral Point in Iowa County was the center of a rough-and-tumble lead-mining region. The first miners wintered in hillside dugouts, dubbed 'badger holes', thus coining Wisconsin's nickname of Badger State. Later came the Cornish, among the best hard-rock miners in the world. It is their squat homes that are magnificently preserved along Shakerag Street, where John Sheldon opened the first federal land office in 1834, and did literally a 'land office' business. Today such Cornish specialties as pasties and saffron buns are still available at area restaurants and bakeries.

71 (right) Along Route 60 near Wauzeka in Crawford County. The epitome of rural Wisconsin: fine farm-to-market road bisecting rolling hills populated with Holstein cows and punctuated by a good red barn.

72 The jewelled shooting star (*Dodecatheon amethystinum*) is found only on bluffs along the Mississippi and La Crosse Rivers, as here in Wyalusing State Park at the confluence of the Wisconsin River and Mississippi in Grant County. A more common species (*D. Meadia*) is to be found in low prairies, woods, and along railroads throughout southern Wisconsin. Memorial Day is its peak time of bloom.

73 *(right)* Near where the Wisconsin River flows into the Mississippi, to a place called Prairie du Chien, came trappers, entrepreneurs, and soldiers of many nations: France, Britain, Spain, and the newborn United States. Here the fur trader Hercules Dousman came in 1826, and from the glistening pelts of beaver he amassed the fortune that built Villa Louis. The great Victorian mansion and its sculptured grounds—now lavishly restored—depict the pinnacle of life in frontier Wisconsin.

74 Sunset Orchard near Richland Center. Twice a year pilgrims from the city make their way to the colorful apple orchards of Richland County, once in the spring when the fragrant blossoms are at their peak, again in the fall when the trees are heavy with flavorful fruit.

75 A tunnel through a big hill along the Elroy-Sparta trail. Hundreds of miles of abandoned railroad grades have been turned into public hiking and biking trails by the Wisconsin Department of Natural Resources. If you rode your bike at ten miles an hour eight hours a day for six days a week, you could ride for a month without following the same trail twice.

76 *(left)* An Amish buggy contrasts sharply with a typical modern Wisconsin state highway just south of Tomah. Clusters of people who dare to be different have found havens in parts of liberal Wisconsin.

77 Resembling for all the world an Alpine or Bavarian village, Ontario nestles in the Driftless Area hills around Wildcat Mountain State Park on the border of Monroe and Vernon Counties.

78 *(left)* A Wisconsin tobacco shed near Wilton in Monroe County signifies the role of the state in supplying wrappers for fragrant cigars.

79 A warm sun melts the lingering nighttime frost in this rural scene in Monroe County.

80 *(left)* A phenomenal wheat production in Wisconsin between 1850 and the 1880s was accompanied by a great growth in gristmills and then in flour mills. With the shift in wheat-growing to the west, milling rapidly disappeared, to be preserved only in such isolated spots as this still-operational Dell's Mill near Augusta in Eau Claire County.

81 Spotted here in Jackson County, the whitetail deer (*Odocoileus virginianus*) is Wisconsin's state animal. Axe, plow, and gun had so decimated the Wisconsin herd by 1925 that the Conservation Department closed the hunting season. Today the sight of deer in Wisconsin woodlands is as common as that of elk in Yellowstone National Park.

82 *(left)* Horses grazing in a field along Route 27 in Eau Claire County.

83 A lookout tower atop Blue Mound State Park in southwestern Wisconsin provides a panorama of Wisconsin's Driftless Terrain, the land the last glacier neglected. Sandstone castles and mural escarpments punctuate the skyline. Springs gush forth from the great maws of grotesque crags. To cruise these precipitous slopes and valley clefts, and to know that everything around and underneath has been from prehistoric times as unaltered as the stars overhead—this gives ballast to minds adrift on change. You can catch, if you will, in the haze of these mellowing hills, a glimpse of eternity.

84 'As you can see, we've got a lot of pleasures of a particular kind in Wisconsin. We like the sun coming up over a lake in the morning.' Sunrise along Lake Michigan in Door County.